Contemporary Hispanic Americans

OSCAR DE LA RENTA

BY
LOUIS CARRILLO

RSVP
RAINTREE
STECK-VAUGHN
P U B L I S H E R S
The Steck-Vaughn Company

Austin, Texas

Published by Raintree Steck-Vaughn, an imprint of Steck-Vaughn Company.
Produced by Mega-Books, Inc.
Design and Art Direction by Michaelis/Carpelis Design Associates.
Cover photo: ©Carol Halebian/Gamma-Liaison

Library of Congress Cataloging-in-Publication Data
Carillo, Louis.
  Oscar de la Renta/by Louis Carrillo.
    p.   cm.—(Contemporary Hispanic Americans)
  Includes bibliographical references and index.
  Summary: Narrates the story of the Dominican-American who had studied art in Spain but gave up painting in order to pursue a career as a fashion designer.
  ISBN 0-8172-3980-4 (Hardcover)
  ISBN 0-8114-9787-9 (Softcover)
  1. De la Renta, Oscar—Juvenile literature. 2. Fashion designers—United States—Biography—Juvenile literature. 3. Costume design—United States—History—20th century—Juvenile literature. 4. Hispanic Americans—Biography—Juvenile literature. [1. De la Renta, Oscar. 2. Fashion designers. 3. Costume design. 4. Hispanic Americans—Biography.] I. Title. II. Series.
TT505.D4C37 1996
746.9'2'092—dc20
[B]   95-19537
                                   CIP
                                   AC

Printed and bound in the United States of America.

1 2 3 4 5 6 7 8 9 LB 99 98 97 96 95

Photo credits: J. Guichard/Gamma Liaison: pp. 4, 14, 38, 40, 42; Steve Allen/Gamma Liaison: p.7; Oscar de la Renta Ltd.: p.8; S. E. Cornelius/Photo Researchers, Inc.: p. 11; Rogers/Monkmeyer: p. 12; Reuters/Bettmann: p.16; Arna/Stills/Retna Ltd.: p.18; LeDuc/Monkmeyer: p.21; Nina Leen/Life Magazine ©Time Warner Inc.: p.22; John Chiasson/Gamma Liaison: p.26; Wide World Photos, Inc.: p. 28; UPI/Bettmann: pp. 25, 30, 34; AP/Wide World Photos: p. 33; Courtesy Mattell, Inc.: p. 36; Allen Tannenbaum/ Sygma: p.44.

Contents

Chapter One

FASHION KING

February 6, 1990. Rock music is blaring. Flashbulbs are popping. Thirty-four very elegant models cross the stage. They pose, twirl, pose again, and return to the back of the stage. All the models are wearing outfits created by Oscar de la Renta. Above them, a giant video screen is showing scenes from the life and career of the famous designer.

The room is crowded. The city's business leaders and government officials are here. So are many of the stars of high fashion and of the social scene. The women in the audience are wearing gowns that are every color of the rainbow. Some have been designed by Oscar de la Renta. Most of the men in the audience are wearing black tuxedos.

For close to thirty years, designer Oscar de la Renta has remained at the top of his own fashion kingdom.

Suddenly, the music stops. Everyone is quiet. A very handsome, athletic-looking man takes the stage. He is wearing a dark suit that fits him perfectly. He speaks softly to the crowd. This shy Dominican American is Oscar de la Renta. He is here to receive an award for lifetime achievement from the Council of Fashion Designers of America. After thanking everyone in his lightly accented voice, he returns to his seat.

Then the music swells, and the flashbulbs begin popping again. People are on their feet, cheering and applauding wildly. It is as if they were at a rock concert! Actually the event is taking place at the Metropolitan Museum of Art in New York City. After de la Renta receives his award, everyone walks to another part of the museum—a huge space that could fit an airplane inside it. A large glass wall looks out over Central Park. In the middle of the space stands a small Egyptian building, the Temple of Dendur. The stone blocks of the temple make it look very elegant. The soaring concrete and glass of the museum wing add to its mystery and beauty.

The open space around the temple is usually empty, but today tables are set up for dinner. Waiters rush from table to table serving crab meat soufflé (a puffed-up mixture of crab meat and beaten eggs) and several other delicious dishes. Oscar de la Renta is too excited to eat. Crowds of people surround his table, pouring out their congratulations. The shy designer talks with the guests and thanks them.

Oscar de la Renta's talents have won him many awards and honors, including this 1990 salute from the Fashion Institute of Technology in New York.

Just who is this man at the center of all this attention? Where did he come from? How did he win such an important award?

Oscar de la Renta is one of the world's greatest fashion designers. He was born in Santo Domingo, the capital of the Dominican Republic. He got where he is because of hard work, a will to succeed, and an extraordinary gift for fashion design. A sound business sense also helped with his success. Oscar de la Renta understood the kind of clothes that women needed and wanted. He designed those clothes, and many thousands of women bought them.

Looking back on his career, Oscar de la Renta has much to be proud of. In 1955, while he was still a

These sketches show Oscar de la Renta's elegant designs for fall 1994.

sketch artist, a dress that he designed was put on the cover of *Life* magazine. Also, before he was thirty, he had worked for two of the most famous fashion designers in the world—Cristóbal Balenciaga and Antonio del Castillo.

In 1966, Oscar became the first high-fashion designer to start a boutique line. This was a line of lower-priced, high-fashion clothing that people who were not wealthy could buy in a store. Countless numbers of shoppers were grateful for this lower-priced fashion. In 1967, Oscar came out with his Russian Look—a combination of fur-trimmed coats and hats and jeweled gowns. As a result of that collection, he won his first Coty American Fashion Critics' Award. He won a second one in 1968 for his Belle Epoque Look, modeled after the clothes of the 1890s and early 1900s. Oscar de la Renta's creative designs have set off many international fashion trends.

Oscar's success was not limited to his designs. In 1969, a company called Richton International bought his business. This made Oscar de la Renta the first fashion designer whose company was listed on the American Stock Exchange.

In 1970, the Dominican government honored Oscar de la Renta for his success and because he had helped his native country in many ways. But Oscar de la Renta did not rest after this honor. In 1982, he helped to found La Casa del Niño, a large home and school for poor children. Oscar de la Renta never forgot the people of his country. Contributing to La Casa del Niño was his way of saying "thank you" to the place of his birth.

The Metropolitan Museum of Art in New York is indeed a long way from a simple house on Sanchez Street in Santo Domingo. Yet that is where it all began for Oscar de la Renta.

Chapter Two

SUN AND SAND

Oscar de la Renta was born in 1932 in Santo Domingo, the capital of the Dominican Republic. The Dominican Republic is part of a large island in the Caribbean called Hispaniola.

The Dominican Republic was a colony of Spain until 1844, when it became an independent country. It has a long history and a rich culture. Christopher Columbus landed on Hispaniola in 1492 and claimed the island for Spain. Many people believe that the body of Columbus is buried in the cathedral of Santo Domingo. The Spanish brought many enslaved people from Africa to Hispaniola in the 1600s. Today, the people of the Dominican Republic are of mixed Spanish and African descent.

The early 1930s were a difficult time in the Dominican Republic. A worldwide depression had begun. Many people were poor and out of work. In 1930, an army officer, Rafael Leonidas Trujillo, was elected president. He had been trained by the U.S. Navy and was a harsh and sometimes brutal leader. That same year, a fierce hurricane hit the Dominican Republic. It destroyed many buildings and caused more hardship. The Dominican people struggled to rebuild their country.

Amidst all this, Oscar de la Renta's birth brought his family great joy. His parents were especially happy because he was the first boy in a family of six girls! The family was very close, and the girls enjoyed taking care of and playing with their new baby brother.

The de la Renta family lived on Sanchez Street, which is part of the Ciudad Colonial (colonial city), the oldest part of Santo Domingo. In the 1930s, the concrete houses of Sanchez Street were all attached

As a boy, Oscar de la Renta enjoyed the sun and sand of his Caribbean homeland, the Dominican Republic.

The Ciudad Colonial in Santo Domingo, where the de la Renta family lived, contains many beautiful churches and homes. Some are over 400 years old.

to each other and painted pastel colors: light blue, light yellow, and pink. The older ones were two-story colonial houses with columns and rounded arches. At the time, the streets were paved with cobblestones. Automobiles shared the streets with horses and horse-drawn carriages.

Oscar's father, Oscar Ortiz de la Renta, was a firm and loving parent. The children saw him mainly at mealtimes and on weekends. He worked hard and spent a lot of time at his office. Mr. de la Renta had an insurance business in Santo Domingo. When the business did well, he earned a lot of money. That made him happy. All his children could have new clothes and lots of toys. But during the depression of the 1930s, many people lost their jobs. When people lost their jobs, they could not make regular payments to Mr. de la Renta's insurance company. The business suffered. Oscar's father worked hard to rebuild it. Sometimes he worried, but he did not show it. His daughters noticed the change, however. They had to wear hand-me-down clothes, and young Oscar could not have new toys.

Oscar's mother, Maria Fiallo, loved him very much. Oscar remembers, "Though my mother was strict with me, I always got away with what I wanted." Perhaps he was spoiled because he was the only boy—and the baby of the family.

Maria was an elegant woman who wore beautiful clothes. When her husband's business was doing well, she liked to make special trips by ship to Havana, Cuba, to buy clothes. At that time, all kinds of clothing from many countries were sold in Havana, where the prices were low. Maria dressed Oscar in the fancy children's clothes that she bought there. It could be that his memories of his mother were the first inspiration for his fashion designing.

Young Oscar was a good-natured child. All the children played well together, but Oscar was especially close to his sister Alicia. Oscar was also a very generous boy. There were many poor people in Santo Domingo, and Oscar became friends with a boy from a poor neighborhood. When his friend came

Today, Oscar de la Renta still enjoys returning to his homeland. Here, he relaxes in one of his homes, on the southern coast of the Dominican Republic.

over to play in the afternoon, Oscar always gave him some food that he had saved from his own lunch.

As a child, Oscar spent many happy hours swimming, running, jumping, and playing at Guibia Beach. The Beach was near his home and near the sea wall, called the *malecón*, that ran along the edge of the Caribbean. In the middle of the road that followed the seawall was the Monument to Independence, a familiar landmark to all. Oscar and his friends often played until evening. Then, in time for supper, they returned home—dusty, sandy, and tired, but almost always happy.

Three

DRAWINGS AND DREAMS

Oscar de la Renta showed talent for art at a very young age. Whenever the weather was rainy, he picked up the nearest pencil and began to draw. Drawing made him feel better when he was lonely or bored. When Oscar was old enough to enter school, he was very excited. One of the classes would be art! He attended the Escuela Normal, an elementary school near his house.

Oscar liked school, but he liked some subjects better than others. He did well in literature and history because he had a good memory. In these classes, students often had to memorize famous speeches and poems. Math was difficult for Oscar, but he worked hard at it. His favorite subject, of course, was art. Some of his teachers recognized his talent and encouraged him to draw more. Soon, his drawings could be seen on the classroom walls almost every day.

Students at the Escuela Normal had to wear uniforms.

Now a model of elegance, Oscar de la Renta grew up wearing school uniforms!

The boys wore khaki-colored shorts or pants and short-sleeved white shirts. The girls wore white dresses and black shoes. Not every girl liked the black shoes. Oscar's sister Alicia remembers wearing colored shoes just so she would stand out and look nice.

Oscar had clothing problems of his own. He grew quickly, and soon he was a head taller than most of the other boys in his class. His legs were very long, and he hated the way he looked. To make things worse, his parents made him wear shorts when most boys his age were wearing long pants. Other boys sometimes called him "Stork Legs." It was an interesting problem for a future clothing designer to have!

At home, Oscar's mother encouraged his drawing, but his father wanted him to work in his insurance business when he grew up. Oscar knew that he would not be happy working in an insurance office. In fact, he was becoming aware of a wider world he wanted to explore—a world far away from Santo Domingo.

One of Oscar's favorite relatives was his uncle. This uncle was a lieutenant-general in the Dominican Army. One day, Oscar's uncle took him along to visit a friend of his. She was a beautiful blonde woman with sparkling blue eyes. The three of them sat on her balcony and drank tea. Oscar had never met a woman like this before. She dressed in long, elegant dresses whose colors brought out the blue of her eyes. Oscar thought she looked like the fairy godmother in an illustration from *Cinderella*.

Oscar began visiting his uncle's friend regularly. This mysterious woman filled Oscar's imagination with tales about her childhood in Russia. Her family had been very rich, with a big house, servants, and gorgeous clothes. But the Russian Revolution in 1917 changed all that. People who were rich and powerful under the old government were now in danger. They had to run away. The beautiful woman and her family left their house in the middle of the night. They could take only a few bags with them. It was very cold in Russia, so they chose warm clothes made of wool and fur. Some of their dresses were covered with jewels.

After they left Russia, the woman told Oscar, she and her family settled in Paris. As a young woman, she left Paris and came to the Dominican Republic. She had been there ever since.

Oscar was entranced. Russia! Europe! Paris! It sounded very exciting—so different from Santo Domingo! It was hard to believe the stories were true. They sounded like fairy tales. Little did young Oscar know that, thirty years later, he would design lovely

Some of Oscar de la Renta's elegant clothing may have been inspired by stories he heard as a child. Here, Oscar joins a model on the runway as she shows off a lace and satin gown created for Balmain in 1994.

coats and dresses made of wool and fur, just like the Russians wore. They were worn with jewelry and fur hats. Perhaps Oscar had remembered the beautiful woman's stories when he was designing this landmark Russian collection.

Meanwhile, Oscar's love of art grew. When he was 16, Oscar finally decided that he wanted to attend the Dominican Republic's national art school, La Escuela de Bellas Artes Las Mercedes. His father was against it. The senior de la Renta argued that young Oscar would never make any money that way. Oscar argued that art was important to him, and that he could indeed make a living by painting. Oscar's father warned him that he would end up as "a painter with a big brush"—in other words, a house painter!

Thanks to his mother's help, Oscar finally talked his father into letting him go to art school. Oscar liked art school, and he did well there. But he grew restless. He had never forgotten the stories the Russian woman had told him. He longed to meet people who were different from him and to make new friends. He wanted to see snow and live where the winters were cold. Most of all, he wanted to see Paris, the capital of France. To Oscar, it seemed like an enchanted city from a fairy tale. Now he wanted to see the real place. Oscar would one day live there. But his next home was Madrid, the capital of Spain.

Four

RUFFLES AND LACE

A very happy but nervous 19-year-old arrived in Madrid in the fall of 1951. At last, Oscar was in Europe! His father had agreed to let him go to Spain to study art. Oscar was happy because a childhood dream had come true. But he was also nervous. Would he really become a success? He wanted to prove to his father that he could be a thriving artist. So, he enrolled as a student at the Academia de Bellas Artes de San Fernando—the San Fernando Academy of Fine Arts.

Spain was both familiar and strange to Oscar. The beautiful Spanish buildings were similar to those in the Ciudad Colonial in Santo Domingo. Oscar loved the majestic Plaza Mayor, the wide boulevards, the strolling people, and the late-night dinners in Madrid. However, Oscar missed his family and the sunny beaches. Still, Oscar stayed on in Madrid.

During Oscar's second year in Spain, his beloved mother died. Oscar's father wanted him to come home and join the insurance business, but Oscar's sisters came to the rescue. They sent him money so that he could stay in Spain. But Oscar did not want to depend on his sisters for money. He got a job drawing illustrations of new fashions for magazines. Oscar would go to designers' salons and sketch the new dresses. Then the sketches would be published in magazine ads for the designers.

One day, the famous Spanish designer Cristóbal Balenciaga saw Oscar's sketches. He liked them, and he offered the young artist a job working at his salon in Madrid. Oscar accepted happily. He quickly got to work, sketching the new Balenciaga dresses. These sketches appeared in special catalogs that were sent

As a student in Madrid, Oscar de la Renta enjoyed the city's streets and squares, including the beautiful Plaza Mayor.

Oscar de la Renta with Beatrice Lodge, who is wearing the gown he designed for her in 1956.

to Balenciaga customers all over Spain. While Oscar was working at Balenciaga's salon, he also kept on painting. But an exciting event soon led Oscar de la Renta to put down his paints forever.

Oscar's fashion sketches caught the eye of Mrs. John Lodge, the wife of the United States ambassador to Spain. The Lodges' daughter, Beatrice, was going to attend a big dance and needed a special dress. So Oscar set to work and designed his first costume—a beautiful, puffy white dress. Beatrice Lodge's outfit was a huge success. It even got on the cover of *Life*, one of the most famous magazines of the time, so Oscar's dress got a lot of attention. After that, Oscar de la Renta gave up painting and began working full-time for Cristóbal Balenciaga as an assistant designer. There, he continued to learn about the fashion business.

First, he learned that the fashion business is divided into two parts. Some designers make **ready-to-wear** clothing, which can be bought in stores by anyone. Other designers, or sometimes the same ones, make **couture** clothing. This clothing is made to order for a specific customer, like Beatrice Lodge.

With ready-to-wear clothing, the designer may first make drawings or experiment with cloth on a dress form or a live model. Then the dress is sewn together. Afterward, the dress is taken apart, and the pieces are used to make a paper pattern. In a factory, the pattern is used to cut many copies from cloth. Then, workers use sewing machines to sew the cloth pieces together. The dresses are made in standard sizes. Finished outfits are shipped to stores, where customers buy an outfit in their size. They can wear it right away. That is why it is called ready-to-wear clothing.

The word *couture* means "sewing" in French. The first step in couture clothing is also the designing of the outfit. Then, just one sample is made in the designer's salon. A fashion show is held where a model wears the outfit. Customers may see the outfit at the show, or they may see a photo of it in a newspaper or magazine. Interested customers then go to the designer's salon. There the outfit is made in the customer's exact size. The customer may try it on several times before it is finished, to make sure it fits perfectly.

Because of this special process, couture clothing is much more expensive than ready-to-wear. Oscar's boss, Cristóbal Balenciaga, was a couture designer.

At work, Oscar also learned that there are many kinds of designers. They work in different ways, and they have different strengths. Some designers have wonderful ideas, but they need their assistants to sketch for them. Other designers do their own sketches but do not sew. Still other designers can do everything themselves, including the sewing. Coco Chanel is an example of a designer who could do everything. Yet even these designers have assistants to help them because the work is too much for one person to do.

As an assistant at Balenciaga's salon, Oscar got a lot of experience in fashion drawing. Soon, he was getting more and more ideas for his own designs. But he still had a lot to learn. Oscar knew that Paris was the center of the fashion world. He felt that, in order to succeed, he needed to work there. So he went to Paris, determined to find a job. His second day there, he spoke with Antonio del Castillo, a famous designer from Spain. Castillo was the designer for the company, Lanvin-Castillo. Castillo asked Oscar if he could cut, drape, and sew. Oscar said yes. Castillo offered him a job as his assistant. Overjoyed, Oscar accepted.

Cutting, **draping**, and sewing are what tailors, dressmakers, and some designers do. To make a dress or suit, they first cut the cloth they need from a big

Oscar de la Renta began learning about the fashion business as an assistant to Spanish designer Cristóbal Balenciaga. Here is a suit from Balenciaga's spring 1963 collection.

roll of cloth called a bolt. Next, they drape the cloth. This means that they decide how the cloth will cover the body. Should a skirt be slim or full? Should it have pleats or should it be smooth? After making these choices, the designers then sew the clothing. In sewing, the questions that have to be answered are: What color thread should be used? What kind of stitch should be used? Should the seams (the lines of stitching) show? All this is complicated and takes a long time to learn.

In truth, Oscar did not know how to do any of these things. But he wanted to work for Lanvin-Castillo very much. So when he accepted Castillo's

Today, in his own salon, Oscar de la Renta still uses the skills he learned as an assistant to other designers.

offer, he asked for two weeks to bring his things from Madrid. Then, he secretly rushed to a dressmaking school and asked if they could teach him the year's course in two weeks!

At Lanvin-Castillo, Oscar learned quickly. He sketched for Castillo and helped him design evening gowns. They got along well together because they had similar ideas and spoke the same language. Soon, Oscar was designing the firm's ready-to-wear line. He learned about the special problems of designing clothing that was going to be made in standard sizes and sold in stores. Little did he know this work was preparing him to go to New York, the center for ready-to-wear fashion.

FEATHERS AND FURS

In 1960, Oscar de la Renta made a business trip for Lanvin-Castillo to New York City. At a dinner party there, he met Elizabeth Arden, the owner of a huge U.S. cosmetics and fashion empire. They talked about Paris and New York and about the latest fashions. Neither Oscar nor Elizabeth liked the straight hair and black clothing that young people were wearing at the time. This style was started by the Beats, artistic young people who hung out in coffeehouses. Oscar and Elizabeth agreed that they did like the style that Jacqueline Kennedy, the wife of President John F. Kennedy, was making popular. The First Lady wore simple sweaters and slacks, sleeveless dresses, and Chanel suits with pillbox hats—simple hats that looked like little round boxes. Elizabeth Arden was impressed by the young Dominican designer. She asked him to speak with her if he decided to come work in the United States.

First Lady Jacqueline Kennedy helped define high fashion in the early 1960s, when Oscar de la Renta began his New York career.

By November 1962, Oscar de la Renta returned to New York to try his luck. There Oscar met with Elizabeth Arden, who was now a friend. He also met with the executives of the French design house Christian Dior. Both meetings went very well. The Dior organization offered him a job, and so did Elizabeth Arden.

Oscar had to choose between the two offers. The salaries were almost the same. The Dior name was more famous than the Arden name. Oscar did not know what to do. In Paris, he had met Françoise de Langlade. She was the editor of the French edition of *Vogue*, a well-known fashion magazine. Françoise had told him about Diana Vreeland, a famous American fashion editor. So Oscar decided to visit the famous editor and ask for her advice.

Diana Vreeland advised Oscar to choose Elizabeth Arden. She had an interesting reason. Christian Dior was an established name in fashion. Elizabeth Arden, however, was known more for cosmetics than for fashion. Arden would be more likely than Dior to put Oscar de la Renta's full name on the labels of the clothes he designed. That way, Oscar's name would be associated with beautiful clothes right away. The young designer took Diana Vreeland's advice and, by January 1963, he was designing two collections a year for Elizabeth Arden.

The clothes at Elizabeth Arden were for a certain kind of woman. She might be young or old. She liked elegant clothes that did not go out of style quickly. She was a woman who had money. She traveled often. She attended big parties to raise money for charities like churches and hospitals. She needed simple, elegant suits that she could wear at work and at lunch. She also needed beautiful evening gowns that she could wear to the opera or a dinner party. Oscar de la Renta designed exactly the kind of clothes these women needed. As a result, many Elizabeth Arden shoppers

Diana Vreeland was considered an expert on fashion for many years. She gave Oscar de la Renta some important career advice.

became loyal customers and fans of Oscar de la Renta.

By 1965, however, Oscar de la Renta was becoming restless again. He wanted new challenges. So that year, he left Elizabeth Arden. He became a partner in the Jane Derby company. Jane Derby had a small ready-to-wear business specializing in elegant clothing. Sadly, she died the same year Oscar joined her company. Soon the company's label was changed to carry the Oscar de la Renta signature. The name of the company remained Jane Derby, Ltd. Oscar de la Renta's name replaced hers on the clothing labels.

Now, Oscar was no longer producing couture clothing. But that did not change his designs much. He designed elegant evening gowns for women who could spend thousands of dollars for one gown. Oscar began to think about the many women who could not spend that much money. He wanted to do something for them. So he started a boutique line. This was a line of dresses that were ready-to-wear and were sold in small shops, or boutiques. The dresses in the boutique line were more colorful and daring than his high-priced clothing. They were well made but cost as little as fifty dollars. Women bought so many of these lower-priced fashions that Oscar was soon selling three million dollars' worth in one year!

By the mid-sixties, hippie style clothing was very popular. Everywhere young men were wearing **bell-bottom pants**, wide ties, wild print shirts, and love beads—sometimes all at the same time! Young women were wearing short "baby doll" dresses, **Pucci prints** (swirling lines in bright colors), and **fishnet stockings**. Soon, Oscar de la Renta was designing loose shirts like pajamas in rich cloth with beaded cuffs and minipants (short pants). Later, he would show fringed **ponchos** with skirts or pants. His fringed evening vests had the words *peace, groovy,* and *dig it* on them in rhinestones or beads.

In 1967, two important events happened in Oscar

de la Renta's life. The first was that he married Françoise de Langlade, the French fashion editor of *Vogue*. Oscar loved Françoise dearly. Shortly after their marriage, he was mugged by two men. He calmly handed over his money, but he asked the thieves if he could keep the money clip. "It is a present from my wife," he said. The thieves let him keep the clip and told him, "You're a cool dude, man."

The second important event was that Oscar de la Renta produced a collection that took the fashion world by storm. The collection was full of sweeping coats, fur trim, mixed patterns, and fur hats. This collection, called the Russian Look, won Oscar de la Renta his first Coty American Fashion Critics' Award. This award is given every year to the designer who has the biggest influence on fashion that year.

In 1968, Oscar de la Renta received another Coty Award. His collection that year went all the way back to the 1890s for its inspiration. The dresses featured high necks, long, puffy sleeves, quilted satins (a shiny fabric), rich **brocades** (heavy fabrics with raised designs), dainty laces, and furs. This collection was known as the Belle Epoque Look.

The following year, a company called the Richton International Corporation bought Oscar de la Renta's business. Oscar de la Renta became the first fashion designer whose company was listed on the American Stock Exchange. Before turning forty, Oscar headed four divisions of Richton International: Oscar de la

Oscar married Françoise de Langlade, editor of a top fashion magazine.

Renta Couture, Oscar de la Renta II (the boutique line), Oscar de la Renta Furs, and Oscar de la Renta Jewelry. Though he was head of the divisions, the real control was in the hands of other Richton executives. By 1973, Oscar de la Renta wanted more control of

By the end of the 1960s, Oscar de la Renta was a huge success. Here, he poses in one of his own designs for men.

his businesses. He invested his own money in Richton and gained control of all four companies.

Soon after this, Oscar de la Renta gave women something else wonderful to wear. He introduced his "signature fragrance," which means a perfume named after him. The Oscar de la Renta fragrance is now a best-seller in fifty countries, and has won a Fragrance Foundation Award.

Oscar has received many other honors from the fashion industry. In 1973, he was inducted into the Coty Hall of Fame. He was twice chosen as president of the Council of Fashion Designers of America (CFDA), and received the CFDA Lifetime Achievement Award in 1990.

In all his years, Oscar de la Renta has almost always designed for women. But he has designed some clothing for men. And, at least once he also designed for boys. He helped design the Boy Scout uniform! In 1974, the Boys Scouts of America asked several designers to design a new scout uniform. The de la Renta organization went into action. Oscar de la Renta gave his services for free. All the designers showed their uniforms to the Boy Scout organization. The design they chose was a combination of the ideas of several designers. The results can be seen at any Boy Scout meeting.

Oscar had another interesting assignment in the early 1980s. He designed for a doll! The Mattel toy company asked Oscar de la Renta to design some gowns for their famous Barbie doll. Designing for Barbie was both easy and hard. It was easy because the doll can stay very still for long periods of time. She does not cry out if you accidentally stick her with a pin. On the other hand, it was hard because Barbie is very small. Making very tiny buttonholes and zippers is difficult work. Even so, all of Barbie's Oscar de la Renta clothes are beautiful!

Barbie dolls model elegant outfits designed by Oscar de la Renta.

Six

RETURN TO PARADISE

What is it like working at Oscar de la Renta's New York City salon? At his offices and workrooms on Seventh Avenue, the salon atmosphere is not very glamorous. The furniture and storage are all very simple. There are lots of mirrors. And there is lots of corkboard on the walls, for pinning fashion sketches. Empty cardboard containers of delivered lunches and dinners sit on the desks. Spanish is spoken frequently at the salon. Two of Oscar's assistants speak Spanish. A third one does not, but he does not feel left out. "When I hear *'precioso*,'" he says, "I know we're home free." *Precioso* is a Spanish word that means "lovely."

What is Oscar de la Renta's life like today? It is very busy. His company, Oscar de la Renta, Limited, has expanded into Europe, Asia, and South America. Oscar still designs his own ready-to-wear fashions. In January 1992, he also started designing for a French fashion firm, Pierre Balmain. He is the first American to design

In his New York salon, Oscar de la Renta creates new designs with the help of many talented assistants.

for a French couture house. Oscar sells over $500 million worth of products each year. Every December, he makes a trip to show his designs at department stores across the country. Here is what Oscar de la Renta's yearly appointment calendar might look like:

January–February: In Paris, design spring couture dresses for Pierre Balmain.

March: In Paris, design fall ready-to-wear dresses for Pierre Balmain.

April–May: In New York, design fall ready-to-wear dresses for Oscar de la Renta.

June–August: In New York, design resort clothes (warm-weather clothes for winter vacations) for Oscar de la Renta.

September: In Paris, design spring ready-to-wear dresses for Pierre Balmain.

October–November: In New York, design and show spring ready-to-wear dresses for Oscar de la Renta.

December: Travel throughout the United States showing Oscar de la Renta spring ready-to-wear dresses in large department stores.

Oscar travels so much that he could be considered a citizen of the world. However, he officially became a citizen of the United States in 1970. Still, he has not forgotten the fact that he was born and grew up in the Dominican Republic. He once said, "For me, it is important to go back home."

The Dominican people are proud of Oscar de la Renta. In 1970, Dominican president Joaquín Balaguer named Oscar a Knight of the Order of Juan Pablo Duarte and a Grand Commander of the Order of Christopher Columbus. Many countries give special titles, like Knight and Grand Commander, to people who have helped the country. People who have a title belong to a group called an order. The orders are usually named for heroes of the country. For example,

Juan Pablo Duarte was one of the founders of the Dominican Republic. Oscar was very honored to receive this title.

Oscar de la Renta is also honored to be a family man. In the early 1980s, he and his wife Françoise took a special interest in a Dominican baby who had been abandoned by his mother. Tragically, Françoise de la Renta did not get to see her dream of adopting

Oscar celebrates the first birthday of his son, Moisés.

the boy come true. She died in 1983. After his wife's death, however, Oscar adopted the child alone. Today, Moisés Oscar de la Renta is a happy and healthy 11-year-old boy. And his father is not raising him by himself. Oscar de la Renta married Annette Reed in 1989. The de la Rentas have a home in Casa del Campo, a resort near La Romana, which is on the southern coast of the Dominican Republic. Whenever he can, Oscar de la Renta likes to go there to enjoy the sunshine of his native country and the warmth of its people.

Oscar de la Renta has contributed greatly to the development of his country. His most important contribution is his work for La Casa del Niño (the House of the Child).

La Casa del Niño was founded in 1982 by local people with Oscar's assistance. It is a complex of buildings in La Romana that provides many services to children. There are three main parts. The orphanage houses children from birth to 12 years of age. The day-care center looks after children from birth to six years of age, while their parents are at work. The learning center teaches young people to read and write. Many young people in the Dominican Republic must work to help support themselves and their families. The students go to classes in the morning. Then they go to their jobs in the afternoon.

The children in all the programs receive regular medical care, meals, clothing, and books. These many

Oscar de la Renta surrounded by some of the many children he has helped through La Casa del Niño in the Dominican Republic.

services cost a lot of money, but contributions from individuals and companies pay the bills. The biggest contribution comes from a fashion show held in Puerto Rico and in the Dominican Republic every year. Oscar de la Renta and his organization give their services for free. All the money that is raised goes to La Casa del Niño.

Today, La Casa del Niño can care for up to 500 children—and it is growing fast. There is a plan to build a technical training center that will teach students carpentry, plumbing, electricity, and other trades.

Oscar also contributes his time, energy, and money to charities in the United States. He loves the arts and is an important supporter of the Metropolitan Opera and Carnegie Hall in New York City, as well as Channel 13, a public television station. Oscar is also a key supporter of the Americas Society and the Spanish Institute, which promotes understanding of Hispanic cultures.

Oscar's own work has opened many people's eyes to the rich creative energy of Hispanic cultures. Oscar has always been proud to be a Hispanic designer, and he believes his sense of color and his understanding of women and their fashion needs comes from his Dominican heritage.

Oscar enjoys talking about women's fashion. In one interview, Oscar was asked what he notices when he looks at a woman. Oscar said that he first notices whether the woman is well-groomed—fresh and neat. He likes to see women who look like they take good care of themselves. He also notices details like hair and shoes. Finally, Oscar said, "There is something else I look for, and that is brains."

Oscar also explained that being "well-dressed" means more than just having good clothes. "It's a question of good balance and good common sense, a knowledge of who you are and what you are," he says.

Oscar de la Renta relaxes in the garden of his country home in Connecticut, where he can take a break from the high-powered life of an international fashion designer.

Oscar knows that the same clothes are not right for everyone. He believes people should wear the clothes that suit them best. When asked what fashion advice he would give women, Oscar quickly said, "Know yourself, then dress accordingly."

Oscar de la Renta's words show that people do not have to have a lot of money to look good and dress well. What is important is to stay healthy and well-groomed—to take care of yourself from the inside

44

out. It is also important to know what kind of clothing seems right for you.

In his fashion advice, Oscar de la Renta tells people to know themselves. His success shows how well he followed his own advice. When other people talk about him, they use the words "shy," "romantic," and "talented." When he talks about himself, one of the words he uses is "competitive." Maybe that is the real secret of Oscar's success—the combination of the romantic artist and the smart businessman. Oscar de la Renta also pursued his dreams. He believed in himself. And that belief took him to the top of the fashion world—almost as if it were a fairy tale.

Important Dates

1932   Born July 22 in Santo Domingo, the Dominican Republic.

1951   Enters La Academia de Bellas Artes de San Fernando in Madrid.

1955   Has sketch on the cover of *Life* magazine. Joins the Balenciaga salon in Madrid.

1961   Joins Antonio del Castillo at Lanvin-Castillo, Paris.

1963   Joins Elizabeth Arden in New York.

1965   Joins Jane Derby, Ltd. in New York. His own name begins to appear on clothing labels.

1967   Produces the Russian Look and wins a Coty award. Marries Françoise de Langlade.

1968   Produces the Belle Epoque Look and wins a second Coty award.

1970   Honored by the president of the Dominican Republic.

1982   Helps to establish La Casa del Niño.

1983   Adopts a son, Moisés.

1989   Marries Annette Reed.

1990   Receives the Lifetime Achievement Award of the Council of Fashion Designers of America.

1992   Begins designing for Pierre Balmain, Paris.

Glossary

bell-bottom Pants with legs that flare or get fuller toward the cuff.

brocade Heavy cloth with raised designs on it.

couture Clothing made to order for a specific customer.

draping The way cloth is placed on the body and how it falls.

fishnet stockings Stockings made of thick, loosely woven thread, like fishnets.

poncho A piece of loose clothing that looks like a blanket with a hole cut in it for the head.

Pucci prints Prints with swirling lines and shapes in bright colors, named after their designer, Emilio Pucci.

ready-to-wear Clothing made in standard sizes and sold in stores.

Bibliography

Gross, Michael. "A Fitting with Oscar." *New York*, April 18, 1988.

Perl, Lila. *From Top Hats to Baseball Caps, From Bustles to Blue Jeans: Why We Dress the Way We Do*. New York: Clarion, 1990.

Rowland-Warne, L. *Eyewitness Books: Costume*. New York: Knopf, 1992.

Index